MAK   GE

Also by Denise Levertov, available from New Directions

DENISE LEVERTOV

MAKING PEACE

Edited, with an Introduction, by
PEGGY ROSENTHAL

A NEW DIRECTIONS
Bibelot

Making Peace incorporates poems from 11 previous Denise Levertov books with New Directions: This Great Unknowing (1999), Sands of the Well (1996), Evening Train (1992), A Door in the Hive (1989), Breathing the Water (1987), Oblique Prayers (1984), Candles in Babylon (1982), To Stay Alive (1971), Relearning the Alphabet (1970), The Sorrow Dance (1967), The Jacob's Ladder (1961).

The quotation from Rainer Maria Rilke in "Life at War" is from Letters of Rainer Maria Rilke, Volume Two, 1910-1926. Translated by Jane Bannard Greene and M. D. Herter Norton. Copyright 1947, 1948 by W.W. Norton & Company, Inc., New York, N.Y. Reprinted by permission from the publisher. "An Interim" was first published in Poetry.

Manufactured in the United States of America
New Directions Books are printed on acid-free paper.
First published as a New Directions Bibelot in 2006
Published simultaneously in Canada by Penguin Books Canada Limited

Library of Congress Cataloging-in-Publication Data

Levertov, Denise, 1923-1997
  Making peace / Denise Levertov ; edited, with an introduction by Peggy Rosenthal.
      p. cm.
  Includes bibliographical references.
  ISBN 0-8112-1640-3 (alk. paper)
  1. Protest poetry, American. I. Rosenthal, Peggy. II. Title.
  PS3562.E8876M25 2006
  811'.54--dc22
                                        2005035048

New Directions Books are published for James Laughlin
by New Directions Publishing Corporation
80 Eighth Avenue, New York, NY 10011

A voice from the dark called out,
     'The poets must give us
imagination of peace, to oust the intense, familiar
imagination of disaster. Peace, not only
the absence of war.'

          —from "Making Peace"

Contents

Introduction

"Political poetry is more deeply emotional than any other except love poetry. You must have traversed the whole of poetry before you become a political poet."
—Pablo Neruda

Traversing "the whole of poetry" is a lot to ask. But Denise Levertov had traversed enough of it to be considered one of America's leading poets by the time she wrote the poems of outright political engagement which appeared in her 1967 volume, *The Sorrow Dance*. Although the swelling popular protest against the Vietnam War had already moved other major U.S. poets to write anti-war poems earlier in the 1960s, Levertov had been hesitant to take this step, concerned that poets shouldn't be pressured to write about current social crises. Yet *"if it happens,"* she told a fellow poet in 1965, "if a poet is *brought to speech* of a political poem, it is a good thing"—for society and for the poet as well.

Within the year, Levertov did find herself brought

to speech of a poem about the war in Vietnam: "Life at War" appeared in *Poetry Magazine* in June 1966 and soon became widely anthologized. She continued writing political poems through the remaining three decades of her prolific career. Each of the eleven volumes of poetry which she produced after *The Sorrow Dance* includes poems explicitly addressing current events, with one of these books—*To Stay Alive* (1971)—wholly devoted to political life. The particular issues whose urgency brought her to poetic speech changed over the years, but her fundamental concern was constant: for the human suffering caused by violent or oppressive government policies.

Identifying in her own spirit with this suffering, Levertov felt compelled to engage it as both activist and poet. First drawn into activism by the Vietnam War, she helped organize protests and was much sought as a speaker at anti-war events all over the country. Then, during the 1980s, she was heavily involved in demonstrations against both the nuclear arms race and U.S. complicity in atrocities in Central America. The 1991 Gulf War motivated her to organize a peace group. Always holding the integration of the human person as a highest value, she would have found it impossible to cut her creative life off from these intensely absorbing activities. "My poetry has always sprung from my experiences," she told an interviewer in 1984, "so if my experience was a political one, it was bound to happen that I would write poems out of that."

"It is when I feel the political/social issues personally," she elaborated around the same time, "that I'm moved to write of them, in just the same spirit of quest, of talking to myself in quest of revelation or illumination, that is a motivating force for more obviously 'personal' poems." This spirit of quest continues to draw us into Denise Levertov's political poems, whatever the current crises our society is facing. Every poem Levertov wrote was informed by what she called the "impulse of personal necessity"; no matter what her subject, her creative process was to enlist the highly-honed tools of her craft in following this impulse with utter self-honesty. The result, when political engagement was her focus, was poetry into which we as readers can personally enter, bringing in the public concerns of our own day.

In offering a selection of these poems, I've tried to choose and arrange them as Levertov herself might have done. My models are the two small editions of poems that she compiled—one on spiritual and one on environmental topics—shortly before her death in 1997. In both, as in all her other volumes of poetry, she adopted a thematic rather than a chronological structure. It was her frequent practice, as well, to title each thematic section with the name of a poem included in it. So for this volume, *Making Peace*, the section "Life at War" leads off with poems evoking war's horrors, whether in Vietnam or El Salvador or the Persian Gulf or a threatened nuclear disaster. The works in this section exhibit Levertov's variety of forms and treatments as she continually experimented with how to craft a poetry appropriately responsive to the horror of war. Part Two, "Protesters," moves into poems of communal resistance to violence: the call to protest social evil by nonviolent witness and action. Poetry's own particular role in public crises is the theme of Part Three, "Writing in the Dark," where the metaphor of the "dark" evokes both the evil of one's times and also the mystery of not knowing what good one's work might do. The poems of Part Four, "Making Peace," envision possibilities of healing society's wounds. As anguished as Levertov could become, she retained a deep trust in human goodness, to which she kept returning as grounds for hope.

It is because Levertov did persevere in writing in the dark that we have the poems gathered here. Taken together, they represent the range of what she sought in political poetry. As she put it in one of her many essays on the subject: "A poetry articulating the dreads and horrors of our time is necessary in order to make readers understand what is happening, really understand it, not just know about it but feel it . . . And a poetry of praise is equally necessary, that we not be overcome by despair but have the constant incentive of envisioned positive possibility—and because praise is an irresistible impulse of the soul."

—Peggy Rosenthal

PART ONE

Life at War

Life at War

The disasters numb within us
caught in the chest, rolling
in the brain like pebbles. The feeling
resembles lumps of raw dough

weighing down a child's stomach on baking day.
Or Rilke said it, 'My heart. . .
Could I say of it, it overflows
with bitterness . . . but no, as though

its contents were simply balled into
formless lumps, thus
do I carry it about.'
The same war

continues.
We have breathed the grits of it in, all our lives,
our lungs are pocked with it,
the mucous membrane of our dreams
coated with it, the imagination
filmed over with the gray filth of it:

the knowledge that humankind,

delicate Man, whose flesh
responds to a caress, whose eyes
are flowers that perceive the stars,

whose music excels the music of birds,
whose laughter matches the laughter of dogs,
whose understanding manifests designs
fairer than the spider's most intricate web,

still turns without surprise, with mere regret
to the scheduled breaking open of breasts whose milk
runs out over the entrails of still-alive babies,
transformation of witnessing eyes to pulp-fragments,
implosion of skinned penises into carcass-gulleys.

We are the humans, men who can make;
whose language imagines *mercy,
lovingkindness;* we have believed one another
mirrored forms of a God we felt as good—

who do these acts, who convince ourselves
it is necessary; these acts are done
to our own flesh; burned human flesh
is smelling in Vietnam as I write.

Yes, this is the knowledge that jostles for space
in our bodies along with all we
go on knowing of joy, of love;

our nerve filaments twitch with its presence
day and night,
nothing we say has not the husky phlegm of it in the saying,
nothing we do has the quickness, the sureness,
the deep intelligence living at peace would have.

What Were They Like?

1) Did the people of Vietnam
   use lanterns of stone?
2) Did they hold ceremonies
   to reverence the opening of buds?
3) Were they inclined to quiet laughter?
4) Did they use bone and ivory,
   jade and silver, for ornament?
5) Had they an epic poem?
6) Did they distinguish between speech and singing?

1) Sir, their light hearts turned to stone.
   It is not remembered whether in gardens
   stone lanterns illumined pleasant ways.
2) Perhaps they gathered once to delight in blossom,
   but after the children were killed
   there were no more buds.
3) Sir, laughter is bitter to the burned mouth.
4) A dream ago, perhaps. Ornament is for joy.
   All the bones were charred.
5) It is not remembered. Remember,
   most were peasants; their life
   was in rice and bamboo.
   When peaceful clouds were reflected in the paddies
   and the water buffalo stepped surely along terraces,
   maybe fathers told their sons old tales.
   When bombs smashed those mirrors
   there was time only to scream.
6) There is an echo yet
   of their speech which was like a song.
   It was reported their singing resembled
   the flight of moths in moonlight.
   Who can say? It is silent now.

Thinking about El Salvador

Because every day they chop heads off
I'm silent.
In each person's head they chopped off
was a tongue,
for each tongue they silence
a word in my mouth
unsays itself.

From each person's head two eyes
looked at the world;
for each gaze they cut
a line of seeing unwords itself.

Because every day they chop heads off
no force
flows into language,
thoughts
think themselves worthless.

No blade of *machete*
threatens my neck,
but its muscles
cringe and tighten,
my voice
hides in its throat-cave
ashamed to sound
            into that silence,
the silence

of raped women,
of priests and peasants,
teachers and children,

of all whose heads every day
float down the river
and rot
and sink,
not Orpheus heads
still singing, bound for the sea,
but mute.

The vultures thrive,
clustered in lofty blue above
refuse-dumps where humans too
search for food, dreading
what else may be found.
Noble their wingspread,
hideous their descent
to those who know
what they may feast on:
sons, daughters.
And meanwhile,
the quetzal, bird of life, gleaming
green, glittering red, is driven
always further, higher,
into remote
ever-dwindling forests.

News Report, September 1991

*"What you saw was a
bunch of trenches with
arms sticking out."*
"Plows mounted on
tanks. Combat
earthmovers."
"Defiant."
"Buried."
"Carefully planned and
rehearsed."
*"When we
went through there wasn't
anybody left."*
"Awarded
Silver Star."
"Reporters
banned."
"Not a single
American killed."
"Bodycount
impossible."
*"For all I know,
thousands,* said
Colonel Moreno."
*"What you
saw was a bunch of
buried trenches
with people's
arms and things
sticking out."*

"Secretary Cheney
made no mention."
"Every single American
was inside
the juggernaut
impervious
to small-arms
fire." *"I know
burying people
like that sounds
pretty nasty,* said
Colonel Maggart,
But . . . ."
"His force buried
about six hundred
and fifty
in a thinner line
of trenches."
*"People's arms
sticking out."*
"Every American
inside."
"The juggernaut."
*"I'm not
going to sacrifice
the lives
of my soldiers,*
Moreno said, *it's not
cost-effective."*
*"The tactic was designed
to terrorize,*
Lieutenant Colonel Hawkins
said, who helped
devise it."

"Schwartzkopf's staff
privately
estimated fifty to seventy
thousand killed
in the trenches."
"Private Joe Queen was
awarded
a Bronze Star for burying
trenches with his
earthmover."
"Inside
the juggernaut."
"Impervious."
*"A lot of the guys
were scared,* he said,
*but I
enjoyed it."*
*"A bunch of
trenches. People's
arms and things
sticking out."*
"Cost-effective."

The Cry

Dedicated to Jonathan Schell

No pulsations
        of passionate rhetoric
                suffice
in this time
      in this time
            this time
we stammer in
        stammering dread
                or
parched, utter
        silence
           from
mouths gaping to
        'Aayy!'—
            this time when
in dense fog
      groping
        groping or simply standing
by mere luck balanced
          still
            on the
swaying
    aerial catwalk of
          survival
we've approached
        the last
           the last choice:
shall we
      we and our kindred
           we and

the sibling lives,
                    animal,
                              vegetable,
we've lorded it over,
                    the powers we've
                                   taken in thrall,
waters,
        earths,
                airs,
shall they
          shall we
                    by our own hand
undo our
         being,
               their being,
erase
      is
         and *was*
along with
           will be?
                      Nothing
for eloquence
              no rhetoric
                          fits
that *unrendering*,
                    voiding,
                             dis-
assemblement—If
                 by luck
                         chance
grace perhaps
              able
                   even now
to turn

to turn away from
that dis-
solution—
only, O
maybe
some wholly
holy
holy
unmerited call:
bellbird
in branch of
snowrose
blossoming
newborn cry
demanding
with cherubim
and seraphim
eternity:
being:
milk:

Between the fear
of the horror of Afterwards
and the despair
in the thought of no Afterwards,
we move abraded,
each gesture scraping us
on the millstones.

In dream
there was an Afterwards:
    the unknown device—
        a silver computer as big as a-
        block of offices at least,
                    floating
        like Magritte's castle on its rock, aloft
        in blue sky–
    did explode,
             there was
        a long moment of cataclysm,
                  light
of a subdued rose-red suffused
all the air before
a rumbling confused darkness ensued,
but
I came to,
        face down,
            and found
my young sister alive near me,
and knew my still younger brother
and our mother and father
               were close by too,

and, passionately relieved, I
comforted my shocked sister,
                              still not daring
to raise my head,
only stroking and kissing her arm,
afraid to find devastation around us
though we, all five of us,
seemed to have survived–and I readied myself
to take rollcall: 'Paul Levertoff? Beatrice Levertoff?'

And then in dream–not knowing
if this device, this explosion, were radioactive or not,
but sure that where it had centered
there must be wreck, terror,
fire and dust–
the millstones
commenced their grinding again,

and as in daylight
again we were held between them, cramped,
scraped raw by questions:

perhaps, indeed, we were safe; perhaps
no worse was to follow?–but . . .
what of our gladness, when there,
                where the core of the strange
                roselight had flared up
                out of the detonation of brilliant
                angular silver,
there must be others, others in agony,
and as in waking daylight,
the broken dead?

The News and a Green Moon. July 1994.

The green moon, almost full.
Huge telescopes are trained on catastrophe:
comet fragments crash into Jupiter, gouging
craters gleeful astronomers say are bigger than Earth
(or profound displacements, others claim—tunnels, if you will—
in that planet's gaseous insubstantiality).

Visualize that. Visualize the News. The radio
has an hour to deliver so much. Cooperate.
Two thirds of what's left of Rwanda's people after the massacres
milling about in foodless, waterless camps.
Or not milling about, because they're dying

or dead. The green moon, or maybe
when it rises tomorrow in Rwanda or Zaire it will look
white, yellow, serenely silver. Here in the steamy gray
of heatwave dusk it's green as lime. Twenty five years ago
absurd figures, Michelin tire logos, bounced on the moon, whitely.

An audio report from Haiti: Voodoo believers
scrub themselves frantically under a waterfall,
wailing and shouting—you can hear the water behind them.
A purification ritual. Not a response to astronomical events
but to misery. Names change, the Tonton Macoute not mentioned

of late, but misery's tentacles don't relax. Babies now
(as the mike moves on), more wailing, no shouting, a hospital,
mothers and nuns sing hymns, there's not much food to give out.
Young men's bodies, hands tied behind them, litter the streets
of Port au Prince. (As rivers and lakes

in Africa have been littered recently, and not long ago in Salvador—
a familiar item of News.) The crowded boats (again) set out,

sink or are turned back. There could be, a scientist says
(the program returns to Jupiter) an untracked comet any time
heading for Earth. No way to stop it. Meanwhile

an aging astronaut says he regrets we're not sending men to Mars,
that would be progress, he thinks, a mild-mannered man, he thinks
too much has been spent on Welfare, all his devotion given to
    leaving
uncherished Earth behind, none to some one particular field or tree
and whatever knows it as home, none to the human past either,

certainly none to sacred mountains and wells or nontechnological
orders of knowledge. And meanwhile I'm reading Leonardo
    Sciascia's
furious refinements of ironic analysis, mirrored pathways
of the world's corruption in Sicily's microcosm. I feel the weight
of moral torpor; the old buoyant will for change that found me
    actions

to reflect itself (as the moon finds mirrors in seas and puddles)
butts its head on surfaces that give back no image. Slowly, one speck
to a square meter, cometary dust, continually as if from an
    inexhaustible
talcum shaker, falls unseen, adding century by century its increment
to Earth's burden. Covered in that unseen dust I'm peering up to
    see

the haze of green radiance the moon gives off this night, this one
    quick
breath of time. No lunamancy tells me its significance, if it has one.
It is beautiful, a beryl, a disk of soft jade melting
into its own light. So silent.
And earth's cries of anguish almost audible.

They speak of the art of war,
but the arts
draw their light from the soul's well,
and warfare
dries up the soul and draws its power
from a dark and burning wasteland.
When Leonardo
set his genius to devising
machines of destruction he was not
acting in the service of art,
he was suspending
the life of art
over an abyss,
as if one were to hold
a living child out of an airplane window
at thirty thousand feet.

The Certainty

They have refined the means of destruction,
abstract science almost visibly shining,
it is so highly polished. Immaterial weapons
no one could ever hold in their hands
streak across darkness, across great distances,
threading through mazes to arrive
at targets that are concepts—

But one ancient certainty
remains: war
means blood spilling from living bodies,
means severed limbs, blindness, terror,
means grief, agony, orphans, starvation,
prolonged misery, prolonged resentment and hatred and guilt,
means all of these multiplied, multiplied,
means death, death, death and death.

PART TWO

Protesters

Candles in Babylon

Through the midnight streets of Babylon
between the steel towers of their arsenals,
between the torture castles with no windows,
we race by barefoot, holding tight
our candles, trying to shield
the shivering flames, crying
'Sleepers Awake!'
                    hoping
the rhyme's promise was true,
that we may return
from this place of terror
home to a calm dawn and
the work we had just begun.

The Love of Morning

It is hard sometimes to drag ourselves
back to the love of morning
after we've lain in the dark crying out
O God, save us from the horror. . . .

God has saved the world one more day
even with its leaden burden of human evil;
we wake to birdsong.
And if sunlight's gossamer lifts in its net
the weight of all that is solid,
our hearts, too, are lifted,
swung like laughing infants;

but on gray mornings,
all incident—our own hunger,
the dear tasks of continuance,
the footsteps before us in the earth's
belovéd dust, leading the way—all,
is hard to love again
for we resent a summons
that disregards our sloth, and this
calls us, calls us.

The Altars in the Street

On June 17th, 1966, The New York Times
reported that, as part of the Buddhist cam-
paign of non-violent resistance, Viet-Namese
children were building altars in the streets
of Saigon and Hue, effectively jamming
traffic.

Children begin at green dawn nimbly to build
topheavy altars, overweighted with prayers,
thronged each instant more densely

with almost-visible ancestors.
Where tanks have cracked the roadway
the frail altars shake; here a boy

with red stumps for hands steadies a corner,
here one adjusts with his crutch the holy base.
The vast silence of Buddha overtakes

and overrules the oncoming roar
of tragic life that fills alleys and avenues;
it blocks the way of pedicabs, police, convoys.

The hale and maimed together
hurry to construct for the Buddha
a dwelling at each intersection. Each altar

made from whatever stones, sticks, dreams, are at hand,
is a facet of one altar; by noon
the whole city in all its corruption,

all its shed blood the monsoon cannot wash away,
has become a temple,
fragile, insolent, absolute.

Living on the rim
of the raging cauldron, disasters

witnessed but
not suffered in the flesh.

The choice: to speak
or not to speak.
We spoke.

Those of whom we spoke
had not that choice.

At every epicenter, beneath
roar and tumult,

enforced:
their silence.

Psalm: People Power at the Die-in

Over our scattered tents by night
lightning and thunder called to us.

Fierce rain blessed us,
catholic, all-encompassing.

We walked through blazing morning
into the city of law,

of corrupt order, of invested power.

By day and by night
we sat in the dust,

on the cement pavement we sat down and sang.

In the noon of a long day, sharing the work of the play,
we died together, enacting

the death by which all
shall perish unless we act.

•

Solitaries drew close, releasing
each solitude into its blossoming.

We gave to each other the roses
of our communion–

A culture of gardens, horticulture not agribusiness,
arbors among the lettuce, small terrains.

·

When we tasted the small, ephemeral
harvest of our striving,

great power flowed from us,
luminous, a promise. Yes! . . .

great energy flowed from solitude,
and great power from communion.

Dom Helder Camara at the Nuclear Test Site

Dom Helder, octagenarian wisp
of human substance arrived from Brazil,
raises his arms and gazes toward
a sky pallid with heat, to implore
'Peace!'
       —then waves a 'goodbye for now'
to God, as to a *compadre*.
'The Mass is over, go in peace
to love and serve the Lord': he walks
down with the rest of us to cross
the cattle-grid, entering forbidden ground
where marshals wait with their handcuffs.

After hours of waiting,
penned into two wire-fenced enclosures, sun
climbing to cloudless zenith, till everyone
has been processed, booked, released to trudge
one by one up the slope to the boundary line
back to a freedom that's not so free,
we are all reassembled. We form
two circles, one contained in the other, to dance
clockwise and counterclockwise
like children in Duncan's vision.
But not to the song of ashes, of falling:
we dance in the unity that brought us here,
instinct pulls us into the ancient
rotation, symbol of continuance.
Light and persistent as tumbleweed,
but not adrift, Dom Helder, too,
faithful pilgrim, dances,
dances at the turning core.

PART THREE

Writing in the Dark

I have been listening, years now,
to last breaths—martyrs dying
passionately
            in open blood,
            in closed cells:

to screams and surprised silence
of children torn from green grass
into the foul bite
                of the great mower.

From a long way off
I listen, I look
with the eyes and ears concealed within me.
Ears and eyes of my body
know as I know:
I have no vocation to join the nameless great,

only to say to others, Watch! Hear them!
Through them alone
we keep our title, *human,*

word like an archway, a bridge, an altar.
(Sworn enemies
answering phrase to phrase,
used to sing in the same key, imagine!—
used to pick up the furious song and
sing it through
to the tonic resting place, the chord,
however harsh,
of resolution.)

Nowadays
I begin to hear a new sound:

a leaf seems as it slowly
twirls down
earthward
to hum,

a candle, silently
melting beneath its flame,
seems to implore
attention, that it not burn its life
unseen.

Because in Vietnam the vision of a Burning Babe
is multiplied, multiplied,
                              the flesh on fire
not Christ's, as Southwell saw it, prefiguring
the Passion upon the Eve of Christmas,

but wholly human and repeated, repeated,
infant after infant, their names forgotten,
their sex unknown in the ashes,
set alight, flaming but not vanishing,
not vanishing as his vision but lingering,

cinders upon the earth or living on
moaning and stinking in hospitals three abed;

because of this my strong sight,
my clear caressive sight, my poet's sight I was given
that it might stir me to song,
is blurred.
            There is a cataract filming over
my inner eyes. Or else a monstrous insect
has entered my head, and looks out
from my sockets with multiple vision,

seeing not the unique Holy Infant
burning sublimely, an imagination of redemption,
furnace in which souls are wrought into new life,
but, as off a beltline, more, more senseless figures aflame.

And this insect (who is not there—
it is my own eyes do my seeing, the insect

is not there, what I see is there)
will not permit me to look elsewhere,

or if I look, to see except dulled and unfocused
the delicate, firm, whole flesh of the still unburned.

Perhaps No Poem But All I Can Say
And I Cannot Be Silent

As a devout Christian, my father
took delight and pride in being
(like Christ and the Apostles)
a Jew.
    It was
    Hasidic lore, his heritage,
    he drew on to know
    the Holy Spirit as Shekinah.

My Gentile mother, Welsh through and through,
and like my father sustained
by deep faith, cherished
all her long life the words
of Israel Zangwill, who told her,
'You have a Jewish soul.'

I their daughter ('flesh of their flesh,
                bone of their bone')
writing, in this Age of Terror, a libretto
about El Salvador, the suffering,
        the martyrs,

look from my page to watch
the apportioned news—those foul
dollops of History
each day thrusts at us, pushing them
into our gullets—
        and see that,
        in Lebanon
    so-called Jews have permitted

so-called Christians
to wreak pogrom ('thunder of devastation')
on helpless folk (of a tribe
anciently kin to their own, and now
concentrated
                in Camps . . .)

My father—my mother—
I have longed for you.
Now I see
           it is well you are dead,
dead and
gone from Time,
gone from this time whose weight
of shame your bones, weary already
from your own days and years of
tragic History,
could surely not have borne.

Witnessing from Afar the New
Escalation of Savage Power

She was getting old, had seen a lot,
knew a lot.
But something innocent
enlivened her,
upheld her spirits.
She tended a small altar,
kept a candle shielded there,
or tried to. There was a crash and throb
of harsh sound audible
always, but distant.
She believed
she had it in her
to fend for herself and hold
despair at bay.
Now when she came to the ridge and saw
the world's raw gash
reopened, the whole world
a valley of steaming blood,
her small wisdom
guttered in the uprush;
rubbledust, meatpulse—
darkness and the blast
levelled her. (Not her own death,
that was not yet.) The deafening
downrush. Shock, shame
no memory, no knowledge
nor dark imagination
had prepared her for.

January—March 1991

Where Is the Angel?

Where is the angel for me to wrestle?
No driving snow in the glass bubble,
but mild September.

Outside, the stark shadows
menace, and fling their huge arms about
unheard. I breathe

a tepid air, the blur
of asters, of brown fern and gold-dust
seems to murmur,

and that's what I hear, only that.
Such clear walls of curved glass:
I see the violent gesticulations

and feel—no, not nothing. But in this
gentle haze, nothing commensurate.
It is pleasant in here. History

mouths, volume turned off. A band of iron,
like they put round a split tree,
circles my heart. In here

it is pleasant, but when I open
my mouth to speak, I too
am soundless. Where is the angel

to wrestle with me and wound
not my thigh but my throat,
so curses and blessings flow storming out

and the glass shatters, and the iron sunders?

Immersion

There is anger abroad in the world, a numb thunder,
because of God's silence. But how naive,
to keep wanting words we could speak ourselves,
English, Urdu, Tagalog, the French of Tours,
the French of Haiti . . .
                    Yes, that was one way omnipotence chose
to address us—Hebrew, Aramaic, or whatever the patriarchs
chose in their turn to call what they heard. Moses
demanded the word, spoken and written. But perfect freedom
assured other ways of speech. God is surely
patiently trying to immerse us in a different language,
events of grace, horrifying scrolls of history
and the unearned retrieval of blessings lost for ever,
the poor grass returning after drought, timid, persistent.
God's abstention is only from human dialects. The holy voice
utters its woe and glory in myriad musics, in signs and portents.
Our own words are for us to speak, a way to ask and to answer.

It's not difficult.
Anyway, it's necessary.

Wait till morning, and you'll forget.
And who knows if morning will come.

Fumble for the light, and you'll be
stark awake, but the vision
will be fading, slipping
out of reach.

You must have paper at hand,
a felt-tip pen–ballpoints don't always flow,
pencil points tend to break. There's nothing
shameful in that much prudence: those are your tools.

Never mind about crossing your t's, dotting your i's–
but take care not to cover
one word with the next. Practice will reveal
how one hand instinctively comes to the aid of the other
to keep each line
clear of the next.

Keep writing in the dark:
a record of the night, or
words that pulled you from depths of unknowing,
words that flew through your mind, strange birds
crying their urgency with human voices,

or opened
as flowers of a tree that blooms
only once in a lifetime:

words that may have the power
to make the sun rise again.

PART FOUR

Making Peace

From the Image-Flow—Summer of 1986

'Only Hope remained there within
the rim of the great jar' (*after
Pandora had let loose disaster
and affliction*).

These days—these years—
when powers and principalities of death
weigh down the world, deeper, deeper
than we ever thought it could fall and still
                              keep slowly spinning,
Hope, caught under the jar's rim, crawls
like a golden fly
round and around, a sentinel:
it can't get out, it can't fly free
among our heavy hearts—
but does not die, keeps up its pace,
pausing only as if to meditate
a saving strategy . . .

City Psalm

The killings continue, each second
pain and misfortune extend themselves
in the genetic chain, injustice is done knowingly, and the air
bears the dust of decayed hopes,
yet breathing those fumes, walking the thronged
pavements among crippled lives, jackhammers
raging, a parking lot painfully agleam
in the May sun, I have seen
not behind but within, within the
dull grief, blown grit, hideous
concrete façades, another grief, a gleam
as of dew, an abode of mercy,
have heard not behind but within noise
a humming that drifted into a quiet smile.
Nothing was changed, all was revealed otherwise;
not that horror was not, not that the killings did not continue,
not that I thought there was to be no more despair,
but that as if transparent all disclosed
an otherness that was blesséd, that was bliss.
I saw Paradise in the dust of the street.

from During the Eichmann Trial

i When We Look Up

> When we look up
> each from his being
> *Robert Duncan*

He had not looked,
pitiful man whom none

pity, whom all
must pity if they look

into their own face (given
only by glass, steel, water

barely known) all
who look up

to see—how many
faces?   How many

seen in a lifetime? (Not those
that flash by, but those

into which the gaze wanders
and is lost

and returns to tell
Here is a mystery,

**a person, an
other, an I?**

Count them.
Who are five million?)

'I was used from the nursery
to obedience

all my life . . .
Corpselike

obedience.' Yellow
calmed him later—

'a charming picture'
yellow of autumn leaves in

Wienerwald, a little
railroad station
nineteen-o-eight, Lemburg,

yellow sun
on the stepmother's teatable

Franz Joseph's beard
blessing his little ones.

It was the yellow
of the stars too,

stars that marked
those in whose faces

you had not
looked. 'They were cast out

as if they were
some animals, some beasts.'

'And what would disobedience
have brought me? And

whom would it have served?'
'I did not let my thoughts

dwell on this—I had
seen it and that was

enough.' (The words
'slur into a harsh babble')

'A spring of blood
gushed from the earth.'
Miracle

unsung. I see
a spring of blood gush from the earth—

Earth cannot swallow
so much at once

a fountain
rushes towards the sky

unrecognized
a sign—.

Pity this man who saw it
whose obedience continued—

he, you, I, which shall I say?
He stands

isolate in a bulletproof
witness-stand of glass,

a cage, where we may view
ourselves, an apparition

telling us something he
does not know: we are members

one of another.

For the New Year, 1981

I have a small grain of hope–
one small crystal that gleams
clear colors out of transparency.

I need more.

I break off a fragment
to send you.

Please take
this grain of a grain of hope
so that mine won't shrink.

Please share your fragment
so that yours will grow.

Only so, by division,
will hope increase,

like a clump of irises, which will cease to flower
unless you distribute
the clustered roots, unlikely source–
clumsy and earth-covered–
of grace.

iv

Peace as grandeur. Energy
serene and noble. The waves
break on the packed sand,

butterflies take the cream o' the foam,
from time to time a palmtree lets fall
another dry branch, calmly.
       The restlessness
of the sound of waves
transforms itself in its persistence
to that deep rest.
    At fourteen
after measles my mother took me
to stay by the sea. In the austere presence

of Beachy Head we sat long hours
close to the tideline. She read aloud
from George Eliot, while I half-dozed
and played with pebbles. Or I read
to myself Richard Jefferies'
The Story of My Heart, which begins

in such majesty.
      I was mean and grouchy
much of the time, but she forgave me,

and years later remembered
only the peace of that time.

The quiet there is
in listening.
                    Peace could be

that grandeur, that dwelling
in majestic presence, attuned
to the great pulse.

ix

But on a hill in Dorset
    while the bells of Netherbury
    pealed beyond the grove of
    great beeches,
            and Herefords,
    white starred on tawny ample brows,
    grazed, slow, below us,
                only days ago,
Bet said:
There was a dream I dreamed always
over and over,

a tunnel
and I in it, distraught

and great dogs blocking
each end of it

and I thought I must
always go on
dreaming that dream,
trapped there,

but Mrs. Simon listened
and said

why don't you sit down
in the middle of the tunnel
quietly:

imagine yourself
quiet and intent sitting there,
not running from blocked
exit to blocked exit.

Make a place for yourself
in the darkness
and wait there. *Be* there.

The dogs
will not go away.
They must be transformed.

Dream it that way.
Imagine.

Your being, a fiery stillness,
is needed to TRANSFORM
the dogs.

And Bet said to me:
Get down into your well,

it's your well

go deep into it

into your own depth as into a poem.

A voice from the dark called out,
        'The poets must give us
imagination of peace, to oust the intense, familiar
imagination of disaster. Peace, not only
the absence of war.'
                But peace, like a poem,
is not there ahead of itself,
can't be imagined before it is made,
can't be known except
in the words of its making,
grammar of justice,
syntax of mutual aid.
                A feeling towards it,
dimly sensing a rhythm, is all we have
until we begin to utter its metaphors,
learning them as we speak.
                A line of peace might appear
if we restructured the sentence our lives are making,
revoked its reaffirmation of profit and power,
questioned our needs, allowed
long pauses . . .
                A cadence of peace might balance its weight
on that different fulcrum; peace, a presence,
an energy field more intense than war,
might pulse then,
stanza by stanza into the world,
each act of living
one of its words, each word
a vibration of light—facets
of the forming crystal.

Notes

"Thinking about El Salvador," page 6: The title originally included the date 1982, but alas, the death squads and the army continue the slaughter, with U.S. help.—*D.L., 1984*

"Land of Death-Squads," page 8: My source was a quotation in a review of Jonathan Maslow's *Bird of Life, Bird of Death*. His focus in that book was on Guatemala, where he sought the quetzal in the dwindling forests; but of course the bodies of the "disappeared" have been found in garbage dumps in other countries as well.—*D.L., 1989*

"News Report, September 1991," page 9: This is a found poem, collaged from *The Seattle Times* of September 12, 1991.—*D.L., 1992*

"The Cry," page 12: At the height of the Cold War's nuclear arms race, Jonathan Schell, to whom the poem is dedicated, wrote the 1982 bestseller *The Fate of the Earth*, a chilling evocation of what nuclear war would do to our planet.

"Psalm: People Power at the Die-in," page 28: In 1978, Levertov participated in a three-day sit-in at the Nuclear Regulatory Commission in Washington, D.C. to protest construction of a nuclear power plant in Seabrook, New Hampshire. One event staged by the protesters was a "die-in," in which they simulated the gruesome mass deaths that would result from a nuclear accident.

"Dom Helder Camara at the Nuclear Test Site," page 30: Anti-nuclear protests have been held at the Nevada Nuclear Test Site since the 1980s. At this 1991 protest, Levertov participated along with the Brazilian Catholic Archbishop, Dom Helder Camara.

"Perhaps No Poem But All I Can Say And I Cannot Be Silent," page 37: The "libretto about El Salvador" became "El Salvador: Requiem and Invocation," set to music by Newell Hendricks and performed at Harvard University in May 1983. Levertov's text was published in her *A Door in the Hive* (1989).

"During the Eichmann Trial: i. When We Look Up," page 49: In 1961, former Nazi official Adolf Eichmann was tried in an Israeli court for his role in carrying out the Holocaust. The trial was televised internationally; Eichmann testified from within a bulletproof glass booth.

"An Interim: iv. Peace as grandeur," page 54, and "Staying Alive: Part III, ix. But on a hill in Dorset," page 56, are from Levertov's 60-page 1971 poem, "Staying Alive," a dramatic montage issuing from her exhausting involvement in anti-war activism during the Vietnam era.

Index of Titles and First Lines

Denise Levertov
The Life Around Us
Selected Poems on Nature

As Denise Levertov comments in her brief foreword to *The Life Around Us,* she has "shared with most poets in every time and place an ardent love of what my eyes and other senses revealed to me in the world we call 'nature'." Yet in this selection of sixty-two poems chosen by the author "celebration and fear of loss are necessarily conjoined."

The Life Around Us shows us both the eternal renewal of the natural world and its imperilment. "In these last few decades of the 20th century it has become ever clearer to all thinking people that although we humans are a part of nature ourselves, we have become, in multifarious ways, an increasingly destructive element within it, shaking and breaking 'the great web'— perhaps irremediably."

Available from New Directions: ISBN 0-8112-1352-8

Denise Levertov

The Stream & the Sapphire

Selected Poems on Religious Themes

Conceived as a convenience to those readers who are themselves concerned with doubt and faith, *The Stream & the Sapphire* presents a compact thematic grouping of thirty-eight poems, originally published in seven separate volumes. The earliest poem here dates from 1978, and though the sequence is not wholly chronological, "it does," as Denise Levertov remarks in her brief Foreword, "to some extent, trace my slow movement from agnosticism to Christian faith, a movement incorporating much of doubt and questioning as well as affirmation."

Available from New Directions: ISBN 0-8112-1354-4

Please visit www.ndpublishing.com for a complete list of New Directions books, or write for a free catalog: New Directions, 80 8th Avenue, New York, NY 10011.